D1708949

30 DAYS OF

WORLDBUILDING

AN AUTHOR'S STEP-BY-STEP GUIDE
TO BUILDING FICTIONAL WORLDS

A TREVENA

30 Days of Worldbuilding is also available as an ebook Guidebook.

The content of the ebook is the same. It offers a more portable version of this workbook, and simply requires you to provide your own space for notes.

AUTHOR GUIDES SERIES

30 DAYS OF WORLDBUILDING
An Author's Step-by-Step Guide to Building Fictional Worlds

HOW TO DESTROY THE WORLD
An Author's Guide to Writing Dystopia and Post-Apocalypse

FROM SANCTITY TO SORCERY
An Author's Guide to Building Belief Structures and Magic Systems

HOW TO CREATE HISTORY
An Author's Guide to Creating History, Myths, and Monsters

COMPLETE WORLDBUILDING
An Author's Step-by-Step Guide to Building Fictional Worlds

angelinetrevena.co.uk/worldbuilding

CONTENTS

Introduction   i

Using this Workbook   iv

Worldbuilding Basics   1

Day 1: Genre and Setting   7

Day 2: Draw Your Map   8

Day 3: Water Sources   10

Day 4: Capital   11

Day 5: Landscape   12

Day 6: Natural Resources   13

Day 7: Sapient Species   14

Day 8: Food   16

Day 9: Farmed Animals   18

Day 10: Natural Predators   20

Day 11: Climate and Seasons   22

Day 12: Trade Routes and Travel   24

Day 13: Important Trade Towns   26

Day 14: Education   28

Day 15: Law and Order   30

Day 16: Government Structure   32

Day 17: Economics   34

Day 18: Family Groups   36

Day 19: Gender Roles   38

Day 20: Employment   40

Day 21: Class Divides and Social Mobility   42

Day 22: Religious and Spiritual Belief Structure   44

Day 23: Magic   46

Day 24: Festivals and Celebrations   48

Day 25: Technology   50

Day 26: Medicine   52

Day 27: Weaponry   54

Day 28: Historic Wars   56

Day 29: Social Change and Revolution   58

Day 30: Other Historic Events   60

Bonus: Creating a Magic System   63

      1: Genre   63

      2: Setting   65

      3: Character   67

      4: Society   69

      5: Magical Items   71

      6: Limitations   73

      7: Consequences   75

      8: Working with More than One Magic System 77

A Word on Info Dumping and Learning Curves   79

Ideas Dump   81

INTRODUCTION

I am one of those authors who have been writing, pretty much, since they were old enough to hold a pen. I have a folder of old stories, typed up on an old typewriter, that I don't even remember having written.

I was rarely seen without a book in my hand, and spent every spare hour I had, buried deep in fantastical worlds. I was lucky in that my parents encouraged it. They never told me that I was wasting my time, or to keep my head out of the clouds. They even let me read at the dinner table, eating one-handed.

I was also lucky to have access to a local library, and quickly worked my way through the fantasy catalogue in their children's section. I swept my way through all of the Choose Your Own Adventure books; not only following the adventures of kids— passing into a fantasy world to fight dragons, mounted on their bicycle steeds—but I got to control the stories. I could re-read them over and over, choosing different paths each time, creating a multitude of adventures for myself.

My love of speculative fiction had started young. It was my dad's job to read the bedtime stories each night, all of us huddled together to listen. He often picked books from his own collection which, almost exclusively, consisted of classic sci-fi novels. And so, as a child, my bedtime stories were written by the likes of H.G. Wells and John Wyndham. Looking back, I suspect that *The War of the Worlds* and *The Day of the Triffids* were probably inappropriate choices for children about to go to sleep, but it must have caught my imagination. I will forever thank my dad for introducing me to such tales.

At the age of 16 I finally picked up the Chronicles of Narnia books, reading all seven of them in just five days. It was then that my Narnia obsession began, and it has never waned.

Before starting at university, I worked in an antique auction house. Every wardrobe that came through the saleroom, I would check in the back of it for Narnia. It reached the point that the staff would come and inform me each time they took receipt of one!

When they announced the latest film adaptations, I scoured the internet daily for news. I saw each of them on their day of release, going to the cinema alone for an uninterrupted experience. A pure absorption of them. I can still name the four actors who portrayed the Pevensie children, their names branded into my memory. Yes, the woman who can't even remember her own phone number!

One of my most treasured possessions is an old wardrobe. I bought it from a second-hand furniture shop for just £20. It has moved house with us several times, and has practically fallen apart, with my husband tasked with fixing it back together. Carved into its door is a beautiful rendering of a ship, in full sail, riding the sea. And the serpentine hinges on it are like sea monsters. It is beautiful, and largely useless. It isn't deep enough to hold a standard coat hanger on its rail, and the mirror on the back of the door is so mottled and degraded it hardly reflects anything at all. In fact, it has rarely ever been used as an actual wardrobe, and currently holds my increasingly out of control to-be-read pile.

But, because it looks like it may have once stood in the captain's quarters on board the Dawntreader, I will never part with it.

And, over the years, I have collected other bits and pieces that remind me of Narnia. Including film props, and a good collection of behind-the-scenes and the-making-of books. My obsession is complete, and incurable. All that is left is to find a way to Narnia myself. I'm still looking, and I won't give up.

Despite this, I did stray from my love of fantasy. At university I studied Drama and Creative Writing, and wandered away from magic and fantastical worlds. I can't say why, it just happened. Perhaps I felt pressure to finally grow up. Perhaps my university course pushed me towards literary fiction. Perhaps I simply needed a break from it for a while. I don't know.

After university, as I began to navigate the confusing and cynical world of adulthood, I barely read anything at all. For a long time, I hardly managed a handful of books a year. During this time, I read my first ever Stephen King book. It was, interestingly enough, *On Writing* that I picked up first, and I finished it in just a few days. And so, I was brought back to literature with a renewed desire to read, as well as to write.

Although I've been writing since I was very young, it was never my ambition to make a career from it. I wanted to act. I wanted to be on stage. My whole childhood was filled with drama lessons, singing lessons, lessons in several different forms of dance. I was always performing; music concerts, amateur dramatics, school plays. If there was a spotlight, I was in it.

While I was at university, studying Drama, I discovered that I wasn't enjoying it as much as I'd expected to. I had a long heart-to-heart with myself, finally accepting that the ambition I'd had all of my life, my singular goal, simply wasn't what I wanted anymore. And it was difficult to let go of. This vision had shaped my entire life, my entire personality, and I had nothing to replace it with.

But, I couldn't pretend to myself anymore. And, as I continued with my degree, I came to the conclusion that I didn't want to be onstage, blinking into the spotlight, speaking someone else's words. What I wanted was to sit in the back of a darkened auditorium, watching other people perform my words. I wanted to write.

Even with this revelation, I still didn't imagine myself making writing into any kind of a career. The first Kindle wouldn't come on the market for another six years. The publishing landscape was a very different one to what it is today. Becoming a published author was a pipe-dream. One that seemed to rely far more on luck than any kind of talent. A who-you-know rather than a what-you-know industry. And for a young woman barely into her twenties, and still reeling from losing the footing of the one constant she'd had in her life, it all seemed like an impossibility.

As part of my Creative Writing class, our tutor asked us to write a personal introduction to an imaginary book about ourselves. Much like this introduction you're reading right now. The difference being, in that imagined introduction, I wrote "I can't imagine writing ever being anything more than a hobby for me." When I wrote that, I wouldn't have believed I'd ever be writing one for real.

When our assignments were returned, my tutor had highlighted that sentence, responding with the note "That would be a shame." That single comment began a shift in mindset which, over the following years, led me to this moment right now. And this book, through all those that have come before it.

Inspiration tends to come from the most unexpected sources, at the most unexpected of moments.

And I'm sure that my tutor has no idea of the impact she had. Of the wheels she set into motion. Of the future she helped to craft. She dropped a small pebble into a pool, and its ripples are still radiating outwards.

USING THIS WORKBOOK

If you're looking to build your first fictional world, and you're not sure where to start, this is the book for you. If you'd like to deepen and expand your world, this is the book for you. If you find the idea of worldbuilding daunting, and you've been putting off even starting your world, this is definitely the book for you.

This workbook is broken into 30 easy, manageable prompts for you to complete. If you work your way through, simply completing one prompt per day, by the end of the month, you will have a strong, solid basis to your world. From there, you can grow it more.

This list of worldbuilding prompts is not, by any means, exhaustive. Depending on your genre, your story, your characters, and the world you need to create for them, you may need aspects that are not covered by this workbook. Likewise, some of these prompts may not be relevant to you.

Think of it like a garden. This book gives you the foundation to build upon. It helps you to plant the seeds, and offers you seeds you may not have considered planting yourself. But, you'll need to cultivate it, and water it. And, you may have plants of your own that you want to include. A special tree, your favourite flower. You may like to have a pond, or a bench, or a marquee.

The other thing this workbook offers is a safe, singular place to keep all of your worldbuilding notes. It's surprisingly easy to get lost in your own world, and surprisingly easy to forget the details of it. This will become your worldbuilding bible. Your one-stop-shop for everything you need to know about your world. When you come to writing your story, keep this book next to you, so that everything you need to know about your world is in easy reach.

I have purposefully left the work pages of this book as blank as possible, because we all like to work in different ways. Draw pictures, create tables and graphs, or fill it with neatly written notes. Use it in the way that works best for you.

Above all, enjoy your worldbuilding. Enjoy exploring it, and watching it come to life around you.

As a simple human, this may be the closest you'll come to performing real magic. To visualise an entire world from nothing. To pluck things from the air and make them real. To take breath on the wind and form it into something tangible. That is the most real, purest magic I know of.

Of course, I'm being presumptuous here. You may have magical abilities beyond my comprehension. In fact, you may even be a little more than human...

WORLDBUILDING BASICS

While fantasy and science-fiction authors may be doing the heavy lifting when creating their fictional worlds, worldbuilding exists in, pretty much, every genre. To a certain extent.

Whether it's the creation of an imaginary cafe in a real town, or imagining an alternative outcome to an event from history, any book, of any kind, can involve worldbuilding. At the fantasy, sci-fi, and horror end of the scale, the worldbuilding-heavyweights, it may mean the creation of a magic system, or monsters, to slot alongside the real world. Or it may mean building an entirely new world with new species and cultures, right up to an entire universe of planets.

It can become quite the epic task!

Now, I don't know about you, but I tend to get easily overwhelmed by epic tasks. That's why I'm still working up to de-cluttering my house. I just look at the job as a whole, can't untangle where to actually start, and I end up doing nothing at all.

As much as I understand the usefulness and the importance of breaking things down into workable chunks, into simple steps, the ability and method for doing this very often escapes me. Unlike many other people, I can see the wood very clearly. It's the trees I have trouble with.

And this is what this workbook is designed to do. It breaks the task of building a fully fictional world into sizeable chunks. 30 of them (with a bonus one at the end). If you simply complete one task per day, by the end of the month, you will have a whole world to begin writing in, or to continue building into finer detail.

One task a day. That's not difficult or scary, is it?

Worldbuilding doesn't need to be difficult, or complicated. It doesn't need to take forever, or be an excuse for never actually writing the book. It doesn't need to be overwhelming or intimidating. At the other end of the scale, it shouldn't be something that you haphazardly bolt on in a last-minute panic.

As you'll discover through this book, worldbuilding should be tightly integrated with your plot and your characters. Your characters, and their goals, their struggles, their journey, that is the reason your readers show up. That's the reason they keep reading. You can have the most amazing world, but if you don't populate it with compelling, sympathetic, and relatable characters, readers will simply stop turning the pages. Likewise, if you write amazing characters, and put them into a flat, paper world, your readers won't want to walk along with them, or explore with them.

Just as you want your readers to believe in your characters, you want them to believe in your world, too.

1

Let them smell the salt on the breeze, hear the buzzing of the insects. Let them feel the heat of the burning buildings, and feel the oppression of the government. Let them walk every single step with your characters. Invite them in. And invite them to stay. Whether they want to set up home there, or fight to change it.

Your worldbuilding is equally as important as your story and characters. Give your characters somewhere real to live, and give your readers somewhere real to visit. You simply can't separate these things out if you want to write the best book that you can.

So, what are you waiting for? Let's get started with the basics of worldbuilding.

DIFFERENT TYPES OF WORLDBUILDING

There are a few different ways to approach worldbuilding, and which you choose, will depend on your goals, your story, and your genre.

Building a whole new fictional world:
This is mostly used for writing fantasy and science fiction, and involves creating an entirely fictional world from scratch. Somewhere that does not, and never has, existed. It may have similarities to our world, and it may have huge differences. Think along the lines of second-world fantasies penned by the likes of J.R.R. Tolkien or C.S. Lewis.

A real place with an alternative past or future:
This may be taking a real existing place, London, for example, and giving it an alternative or altered history. Imagine if the Great Fire of London had actually been started by dragons. How would that change the world today? Or it may be taking the real-world place, and throwing it into your imagined future. This is very common in dystopia, imagining an unpleasant future for our world.

When using this style of worldbuilding, your map is usually, largely, already done for you. There is likely to be some changes, such as missing landmarks, or different names for places. The extent of the changes would entirely depend on your story, and how different you have imagined the past or future of this place.

A real place with a parallel fictional world:
The other way is to set your story in a real place, and have a fictional world created alongside it, usually invisible or hidden from the general public. Such as in Neil Gaiman's Neverwhere, or Harry Potter, or Hellboy. The fictional side of the world may be tightly integrated with the real world, or it may be quite separate. This would depend, again, on your story.

Whichever kind of world you're building, your objective is still the same: to create a believable world that your readers can really imagine walking around in.

MAP MAKING

One of my favourite parts of worldbuilding is making the map. You don't need to be an amazing artist; a child-like scrawl on the back of an envelope is good enough, as long as it makes sense to you so that you don't end up getting lost in your own world. Which, believe me, is surprisingly easy.

Imagine your characters are travelling from A to B. If, in one chapter, B lies west of A, and then, suddenly, it's south, your readers will notice. Or if B is a coastal town one minute, and a village in the mountains the next, your readers will notice, and it will drag them out of your story. Plus, they will love to call you up on it. They'll email you. They'll message you on social media. And they'll write it in their reviews.

As an author, your job is to keep them in the story. To keep them believing that it's real. To blur out their real world, their real life, and construct a new one for them, for as long as they're reading your book. Glaring inaccuracies will pluck them out of your world. Inaccuracies break the illusion, and remind them that they are simply reading a story. That they're not a hero fighting against a terrible foe. It pulls them back to their own cold, harsh, boring reality. And no one wants that!

And so, at the writing stage, your world map is for you. If you're not confident in your artistic abilities, there are plenty of artists who can create a stunning map to go into the front of your book. At this stage, the map is only for your eyes. Build it out of Lego, build it on Minecraft, mould it from clay, or cake, or whatever. As long as it's useful to you (and you're not tempted to eat it!)

And don't be tempted to simply draw a map and then randomly scatter towns across it. That doesn't happen, it's not believable. Towns are founded in specific places for specific reasons. The main reason being, of course, survival.

So, imagine you're choosing a place to establish a town. What do you need? What considerations do you need to make?

Fresh water source:
The most important and first consideration. Have you ever noticed how many major cities have a river flowing through them?

Varied food source:
Man cannot live by bread alone. Or cake, sadly. Their food source needs to be varied enough to keep them healthy.

Natural resources:
They need enough resources to be able to build their homes, and the things they need. They can also use these resources for trade.

Appropriate land for crops/animals:
The landscape they choose to settle in will hugely impact the kind of food and animals they farm.

Access and security:
Can they get in and out of their settlement easily while still keeping it protected from intruders?

Trade route:
Can traders visit their settlement? Is it on a major trade route, or will they have to rely on people making a special trip?

Predators:
What lives in the woods? Or the mountains? How do they protect themselves against it?

People, by and large, will choose the easiest option for their home, unless the benefits outweigh the dangers or struggles. For example, you might consider it foolish to establish a town in the middle of a dragon breeding ground. But what if just one dragon scale (which could be naturally shed) would sell for a price that could feed a family for three months. Then, it may well be worth it.

NAMING PLACES

There are several different ways to name the places on your map. Remember that it's not just towns and cities you need to name. Depending on how big your map is, you might be naming mountain ranges, rivers, forests, counties, countries, oceans, continents, or even planets.

Just like places on your map aren't randomly placed, neither are they randomly named. They might be named after their founder, or the landscape, or the natural resources, the wildlife, the river or mountain they're close to. They might be named after a local legend; your place names can actually conjure up stories of their own.

Of course, you can backward engineer these things. You can find the name for a place, and then create the reason it was named that. Perhaps no one remembers. Perhaps it doesn't matter to you, or your characters, or your story. As I'll discuss in the next section, you don't need a full and complete history for everything.

There are so many online naming generators. Simply do a search, and you'll find countless. I have two that I favour:

- squid.org/rpg-random-generator
- seventhsanctum.com

HISTORY

Your current world is a product of everything that ever happened there, even if no one in your world still remembers. It's your job, as the writer, to know. To remember what they can't.

I'm not saying that you need to plot out 5 million years' worth of history. Unless you're into that. Some people are. But you definitely need to know enough to understand why things are the way they are. To know enough to effectively create the world, its culture, and values.

As people, we act according to our culture. And each culture is different. And there are variations in that culture. The things we value. The things we see as rude, or polite, or unnecessary. The things we want, the things we avoid. Religion. Festivals. The way we treat our elderly. The way we treat children. The kind of food we eat, and the way in which we eat it. The kind of jobs we do. The differences between rich and poor. The differences between high culture and low culture.

And these things change over time. Invading cultures. Migrating cultures. Important events. A war, or a natural disaster can hugely change a place's culture. Changing what's important to them. Changing the way they live their lives.

And you need to remember that every time something changes, it affects everything else.

There are different levels at which an event can occur.

International events:
Something that affects the entire world. Like climate change, population explosion, the sun dying, zombie apocalypse, etc

National events:
Something that affects the country or large area. Like an economic crash, natural disasters, death of a monarch, etc.

Local events:
Something that affects a town or community. Harvest failure, flood, local elections, introduction of a new predator, a new trade deal, etc.

Individual events:
Something that affects one person or family. Bereavement, loss of employment, loss of home, births, marriages, a lottery win, etc.

It's obvious how an international event affects everything else. I'm sure a worldwide zombie outbreak would affect you and your family. But what about the other way round?

So, imagine a family preparing for a wedding. They order a whole load of wine from the next village. That gives the farmer enough money to finally live out his dream of buying a boat and exploring the seas. When the winter rains come, the lack of the vineyard on the hillside causes a landslip which demolishes the mining town below, which leads to a shortage of minerals, which leads to a shortage of coins, which results in an economic crash.

This is, of course, a somewhat extreme example, but it's an important thing to bear in mind. Think about the butterfly effect, and the ripples you might be sending out.

Imagine your world as a pool. Every event, ever construct, every thing you change or create, is like dropping a pebble into the water. Sometimes, the ripples last a few minutes. Sometimes, a few years. Spreading wider. Affecting more people. Sometimes, those ripples last for centuries.

HOW YOUR WORLD AFFECTS CHARACTER AND STORY

You can also use your worldbuilding to create conflict. Remember that conflict is created when your protagonist's goal is interrupted, or opposed, and you can use your world to do that.

Perhaps the most obvious example is if the protagonist's goal requires them to break the law. But you can use other things too: limitations of magic, social norms and expectations, gender roles. The landscape itself can become a physical barrier, or the weather, or a lack of resources.

And you can use all of this in your worldbuilding to raise the stakes. To increase the tension.

Because your world doesn't exist separately from the people who live in it, and you should create it with those people in mind. They will have opinions about everything. Beliefs, hopes, grievances. Things they love, things they hate. Things they want to change. Things they fight to change.

And these things will differ based on all of their nuances: gender, age, class, religion, etc. So their opinions will be different to the person stood next to them. They may even directly oppose one another. Conflict.

You have to remember that everything comes back to character. You have to remember that you aren't writing a story about a world that happens to have people living in it. You are writing a story about people who happen to live in a particular world.

Worldbuilding. Story. Character. None of these is independent from the others.

DAY 1: GENRE AND SETTING

The genre of your book can have a big impact on its setting, and how much of your world you actually need to map.

For example, a space opera may require an entire galaxy, with multiple planets with their own worldbuilding requirements. Alternatively, you may be mapping a single spaceship.

With epic fantasy, the clue's in the name; you're probably going to be creating a vast amount of world.

However, urban fantasy may only require a single city, or, even, just a single street.

So, your genre can help to determine how much setting you need. Likewise, your chosen setting can help to determine your genre.

If you're unsure, there are many resources online that give a description of all the different sub-genres. Remember that genre requirements can be quite fluid, and that your story may blend two or more of them together. It is also the case that new sub-genres emerge with conventions of their own.

Write a brief description of your setting, and your genre(s) below.

DAY 2: DRAW YOUR MAP

Remember: it doesn't need to be a beautiful work of art, as long as it's useful to you as you write. As long as it prevents you from getting lost in your world.

This will become your absolute go-to piece of information, so it's important that you keep it beside you as you write, and update it as you need to.

Depending on your world, you may need to add more drawings than this space will allow. You may also prefer to create a digital map (you can always glue a printout below). Just make sure you keep everything together, and by your side as you write.

DAY 3: WATER SOURCES

Towns and cities don't simply spring up randomly. There are many essential decisions that need to be made before settling on one place or another.

The most important thing that is needed, in any settlement, is access to fresh water (unless you're writing about non-human characters that have no need for water. In which case, they will need access to their essential element for life.)

Draw the water sources onto your map. Oceans, rivers, streams, lakes, reservoirs. Any bodies of water that might exist in your world.

Also think about where these water sources flow from, and where they flow to. Look at both natural sources of water, and man-made sources. How much has the natural landscape been controlled and changed for their needs? And, what about water sources that no longer exist? Or ones that have been forgotten, or lost underground?

You can make any extra notes about water in the space below.

DAY 4: CAPITAL

Bearing in mind that your people require plenty of access to fresh water, place your capital city, or cities, on your map.

Is it close to the coast? Further inland? Strategically placed for defending your country? Think carefully about its position. Remember that you can reverse engineer this. You can place it, and then add in the reasons for its position afterwards.

Always be asking yourself "why?" Why is it here, and not there? It has to make sense in your world, make sense to your world's history, and make sense to the needs of your people.

Think about its name, and where that name came from. Has it been named after something else nearby, or has something else nearby been named after it? Has it always been called that? And does everyone call it by the same name?

Choose its position on your map, and write some notes about it below.

DAY 5: LANDSCAPE

Think, now, about the landscape of your world.

It can be very tempting to start with a coastline in the east, run to mountains in the west, and then throw every variant of landscape you can think of inbetween.

Different countries can have different kinds of landscapes, but always look at where they border each other. It's very unlikely that marshland will instantly give way to dry wasteland, or that a vast desert will border a deep rainforest.

Think about what's likely, and what makes sense. You want your readers to truly believe in your world. To be able to imagine themselves in it. So, begin by writing what you know. Look at our own world, and the differences between places.

Is the area mostly dry, or wet? Is it lush and fertile, or rocky and sparse? Is it flat plains, or hills and valleys?

The variants of landscape will largely depend on the scope of your map. If your map is a single country, or just part of a country, you won't see that much diversity. If you're creating a whole world, you have more scope. And if you're building an entire universe, you'll be able to go a bit crazy! But, remember that each of your planets still need to make sense. Both by themselves, and where they're positioned in the galaxy.

Create some different landscapes on your map, and use the space below for any notes.

DAY 6: NATURAL RESOURCES

People need easy access to building materials, and materials for making things like pots, and weapons, clothes, and tools. What natural resources exist, and where are they? What is close to your capital? What needs to be shipped in from farther away?

Which natural resources still exist? Which resources have been used up entirely? Are they used in a sustainable fashion? What do your people not have any access to at all?

The natural resources that are used depend on more than just their availability. They are influenced by what tools and skills your population has. They are tied to other issues such as transport, economics, climate, even culture and ethics.

At a base level, your natural resources can determine whether a population thrives, or dies. While people move to be closer to natural resources, they also move away when those resources are depleted or no longer valued.

Add markers for natural resources to your map. Forests, rocks, minerals, reeds, clay. Maybe oil, or volcanic rock, or even things that don't exist in our world. Make any notes in the space below.

DAY 7: SAPIENT SPECIES

What's the sapient species in your world? Is it humans? Is it only humans?

Perhaps there are elves, dwarves, witches and wizards. Vampires, aliens, shapeshifters. Perhaps the animals are sapient, or the plants, or the oceans.

If there's more than one species, do they know about one another? Are they friends, allies? Do they respectfully keep their distance, or wage war against one another?

Think about the distribution of land, and resources. Of wealth and power. Who has what? Who has nothing? And how did they get it?

Write some notes about the sapient species of your world, and any potential conflicts or allegiances between them.

DAY 8: FOOD

What food can your characters grow, or rear, or hunt? What needs to be imported? What can they afford to eat, and what is reserved only for the wealthy?

Consider the seasons and the climate of your world. Consider the landscape. What food can they get when? Are they able to import out of season food? How do they store food? How do they harvest/catch/kill it, prepare it, and cook it? Whose responsibility is it?

None of your worldbuilding elements live in isolation of the others. The issue of food is closely tied to trade, economics, gender roles. It's also important in rites and rituals, religion, and festivals.

There might be beliefs and superstitions, as well as polite and rude behaviour.

Make some notes about the importance of food in your world, and how it affects the lives of your characters. Also think about customs surrounding food, both every-day meals, and special occasions.

DAY 9: FARMED ANIMALS

Which animals are domesticated and farmed? What are they farmed for? Meat? Milk? Skin? Something else? How are they farmed?

Look back at your map and think about the kind of space particular animals need. Do they need acres of grazing land, or just a small pen? Do they need particular plants to eat, or a particular kind of landscape? Can they survive in extreme heat, cold, or other weather conditions, where other animals can't? Can your characters also survive in that landscape?

All animals that are domesticated are chosen for a reason. For their uses, and for their ease of domestication. Large, naturally vicious animals may be farmed, but it's less likely that they'll be curling up by the kitchen fire. So, consider what makes sense in your world, and to your characters. Especially if you're bringing in the element of mythical and fantastical animals.

Make some notes about domesticated and farmed animals below. Think also, about animal welfare. Are animals used for food viewed as little more than raw materials, or are they worshipped and revered? Which animals are kept as pets, and why those animals in particular?

DAY 10: NATURAL PREDATORS

Every place comes with its dangers, but, generally, the pros should outweigh the cons.

Is it worth losing a few goats to mountain lions if the ground is rich and fertile, and the river brimming with fish? Can your people keep the wolves in the woods at bay with a regular sacrificial lamb? Or, perhaps, the wolf pelts are so sought after on the other side of the mountains, and fetch such a high price, that it's worth losing a hunter or two each year.

How is the balance between predator and prey maintained? Remember, once you change one thing in an ecosystem, everything else changes too. Wipe out a natural predator, and you might be overrun with their prey. Introduce a new predator, and you might introduce a new disease that wipes out your cattle. So, be careful with that natural world...

Make some notes about natural predators, and the ways in which they are controlled.

DAY 11: CLIMATE AND SEASONS

The size of your map will determine how much variation you'll be building into climate and seasons. If you're creating several planets, they may all have individual seasons, and climates, and climates within those climates. Remember that there are microclimates, and localised weather phenomena.

Think about the map that you've laid out. If it's very sandy, you're likely to have a hot, dry climate with low rainfall. If it's lush or boggy, your climate will be damp and wet, with a much higher rainfall. Do they have extreme weather conditions, or is it generally temperate and benign?

How is the climate created and controlled? Is it due to a slight tilt in the planet's axis, causing a difference between the seasons, or is it controlled magically, or by the six moons that orbit the planet? It doesn't need to be the same as earth, but it does need to make sense in your world.

Also think about the effect your climate has on the flora and fauna, and on your characters. It will affect what they can grow, what they eat, and when. It will affect the animals they have, and how they build their houses, and what they build with. It will affect the kind of jobs they have, how their day is set out, when their festivals and days of rest are. Right down to affecting their mood.

The climate may have changed over time. It may still be changing. What has caused this? Is it for better, or worse, and is there a way to stop or reverse it?

Do they have beliefs and superstitions about the weather? Little sayings and old wives' tales? Can they predict the weather? How? And how does that affect their lives?

Write down some notes about the climate and seasons in different parts of your world. And remember the pool; you're dropping another pebble in to watch the ripples. Think about all of the things that are affected by the weather, and think about all of the things that the weather is affected by.

DAY 12: TRADE ROUTES AND TRAVEL

Look back at your map and start to think about trade routes and travel.

How do people travel around your map, and how do they transport goods? Small goods, and large, heavy goods like logs or rock. You need to think about how long it takes to travel around your map, and think about how perishable items might be transported.

This will entirely depend on the technology available in your world. Must your characters walk, or ride on horseback? Do they travel by steam power, or in balloons? Do they have fast cars and aeroplanes to get around? Perhaps they can travel at the speed of light.

Look at who trades with who, and find the most direct, easiest, and cheapest route between them.

Also think about the cost of travel. Is it open to everyone? How much faster can those with money travel around, compared to the poorer people? What advantage does it give them?

Ease of travel around your world, and the speed, and the cost of it, will impact migration, employment, family relations. It will impact leisure time and holidays.

DAY 13: IMPORTANT TRADE TOWNS

If your trade routes are long, featureless expanses of distance, then taverns, inns, space ports, or entire towns might crop up along that route, taking advantage of wealthy merchants in need of rest, refreshments, and refuelling.

Where are the markets? Which are the big, popular markets, and which ones are smaller? Where are the everyday goods produced and sold, and where are the luxury, rare, and expensive ones made? Where do people go for the most sought after goods?

Which towns have become more prosperous through trade, and which have been abandoned and forgotten?

Mark the important trade towns on your map, and those that have sprung up along the trade routes. Think carefully about their position in relation to the natural resources: both where those resources are, and where they aren't.

Large, important trade towns will have several routes in and out of them. Consider the security of them, as well as the ease of access. Perhaps there are large train stations or bus stations. Maybe there are huge space ports. Perhaps those with stable room to spare make a fortune on market days.

Keep bringing it back to the character level. Think about how such things impact them.

DAY 14: EDUCATION

Let's move away from the physical world, and start looking at the lives of your characters and the society in which they live.

Are children educated in formal institutions, such as schools, or are they taught at home? At what age does their education begin, and at what age does it end? Think about the stages in between; moving on to different schools, or college, or university.

You also need to consider who is offered an education, and what kind of education is offered to who. Is education equally accessible by rich and poor, girls and boys, in rural or urban communities? Is it open to every religion, culture, race, species? Perhaps the schools are separated by some of these things, and maybe different educations, and different standards of education, are taught to each demographic.

Are children educated to give them the best chance in life, to offer them the opportunity for social mobility, or are they simply prepared for the labour market, according to their social class?

Think about the curriculum. Which lessons are taught? Is the curriculum the same across the whole world, or does it differ by area or by individual school? Perhaps there are subjects that are forbidden, and books that are no longer allowed in schools. How has this affected education, and the lives of the younger generations? Maybe these forbidden lessons are still taught at home, or in underground schools.

Is education compulsory? What is the punishment for not attending school, and is it given to the child, the parent, or both? What is the punishment for learning something you shouldn't be learning?

Is education free? If it is, think about how it is funded. If not, think about who can afford it, and what happens to those who can't. Are there scholarships to be won?

What happens with particularly gifted children? Are some talents revered while others are condemned? Are all children taught in the same fashion, or are their lessons tailored to the way they learn best?

Education is the foundation on which society and the labour market is built. It's important to think about how education has changed over time, and why, and how this shows in the differences between the generations. This gives you another avenue for conflict and tension in your stories.

DAY 15: LAW AND ORDER

Who is responsible for law and order? Who sets the rules, and how are they decided on? And who carries out the role of policing them?

Perhaps there is no formal law and order in your world. Perhaps each community looks after it themselves, setting their own rules, and dishing out punishments.

Remember that, if your map covers more than a single country, or area, then there may be different systems in place across your world.

How is innocence and guilt decided? A single judge, a jury, a monarch, an elder, a council, or some kind of challenge or physical trial? Are trials fair, and are they fair for everyone?

This, again, is a really good way that you can create disparity between different societal groups. And, with disparity, comes conflict: a necessary component of every story.

Think about the punishments, and what kind of punishments are given for which crimes. Are punishments focussed on vengeance, justice, or do they focus on rehabilitation, and forgiveness?

If your world has a police force, think about the hierarchy, and the different ranks. Who can rise to which rank, and how do they get there? Who has superiority over who? And who, essentially, has the final say over everything?

If you have different creatures in your world, and beings with magical and paranormal abilities, do they need different punishments specific to their kind? Do they require specialist cells to hold them? Are there ways in which their abilities can be controlled or stopped? Is this reversible?

DAY 16: GOVERNMENT STRUCTURE

Let's look to the people in charge. You may need to design different governments for different countries, or planets across your map.

Is it a single person in charge; such as a monarch or a dictator? Or is it a group of people? How do they come to office? Are they inherited roles, passed from father to son, or mother to daughter? Are government officials elected, or can they buy their way in? Is everyone able to stand for government? Can everyone vote?

There may be different levels of government, with each level presiding over something different. They may come to office in different ways. They may still answer to a monarch, or single person with the power to pass or reject their proposals. Or, that monarch may be in no more than a ceremonial position, without any real power.

Remember that the person who is supposed to be in charge, and appears to be in charge, isn't always the one making the decisions.

Perhaps there is no government at all, and your people have a different way of structuring society. Maybe the privilege of the role isn't offered first to those with wealth, connections, or intelligence. Maybe the most beautiful rise to the top, or the most athletic, or those with certain magical abilities.

DAY 17: ECONOMICS

What is the main form of currency in your world? Do they trade in money, or do they barter goods and labour? Or something else entirely?

Think about what your currency is worth. How much does an apple cost, a horse, or a house? How much is a day's wages, and how does that compare?

What makes a currency's value increase, or decrease? What might cause an economic crash in your world, and what might the consequences be?

How about the economic structure in your world? Perhaps it's a capitalist society, maybe people hoard money and resources. Maybe it's communist, and everyone has an equal share. Perhaps it's something else. Is it fair and equal, or is the system abused by some?

Where is money kept, and how is it accessed? Think about other ways that wealth may be safeguarded; in the purchase of land, or property, or businesses. Perhaps the purchase of other commodities. Maybe, through doing these things, other people are disadvantaged. Maybe they lose access to a forest vital for hunting and wood. Maybe they lose access to an ancestral homeland.

There's little more personal than money, so remember to keep bringing it back to the character level.

DAY 18: FAMILY GROUPS

How are family groups organised in your world? Do they live together for life, with several generations living in one house, or in adjoining houses? Or do they spread far and wide once they come of age?

Think about everyone's roles in the family, and whether they are mostly matriarchal, patriarchal, or jointly run. Do the older family members have the final say, or is it survival of the fittest?

What part does the institution of family play in your world? Perhaps families are viewed as sacred, and of higher importance than anything else, or maybe families are fractured, and have very few ties to one another. And how do these things differ between the different social groups in your world?

Do children stay with their parents, to be raised into adulthood? Maybe they're sent away at a young age, only returning home once they are independent. Perhaps parents have no more impact in their lives than simply conceiving and birthing them.

Consider the culture in your world, and how it has led to the way families live. Also, how this has changed over time? Perhaps the older generations have a very different view of family then the younger ones. What happens when families subvert the commonly held ideals?

Are there rules on who can marry who? Are couples monogamous? Do they come together through love, convenience, or simply for the continuation of their species?

What happens in your world when families break apart? Think about deaths, marriages, divorce, and re-marriages. Consider step-siblings, half-siblings.

How much influence does the family have? Maybe the law of the family is more important than the law of the land. Perhaps crimes are forgiven if family honour was at stake.

Family groupings have a huge impact on your characters. And, therefore, on the wider society. They often stand as a person's first lessons in socialisation, gender roles, norms, values, morality. What happens if your character doesn't come from a standard family group? What happens if they reject it?

DAY 19: GENDER ROLES

Closely related to family, are gender roles. Within the family environment, who is responsible for which domestic tasks? Outside of the home, how do gender roles play out in wider society; in education, in the workplace, in government?

Which gender-related qualities (or perceived qualities) are revered? Which are seen as weaknesses? And which are encouraged, which frowned upon, or, even, subject to punishment?

Does your world have gender equality, or is one gender held above another?

Perhaps there is a fluidity of gender, and maybe gender isn't determined, or defined, in the same way it is in our world. There may well be several different genders, and these may be changeable over a person's lifetime. How do they change, and how is this decided? Maybe there is no gender at all.

Think about how all of this ties into the make-up of your world. Its culture, its values, and how it affects the individual characters. Especially if they don't fit society's perceived 'norm'.

DAY 20: EMPLOYMENT

What kind of job prospects are there in your world? Which roles are highly sought after, and which struggle to get any applicants at all?

Perhaps people in your world can't choose their jobs; maybe they're assigned at birth, based on their parents' positions, or based on academic attainment. Maybe roles are randomly assigned, or based on a lottery system.

Do people find work close to home, or are they happy to uproot their family and move miles away to find employment?

Think, also, about the work environment, and the rights, or lack of rights, offered to employees. Do they have company benefits, pensions, discounts? Are they allowed holidays, sick pay, written warnings before being fired?

Also consider the work-life balance. How much free time do people have? Maybe a lack of leisure time is used to control the population. Maybe work is viewed as secondary in importance to family time, or the pursuit of hobbies and passions (that would be a wonderful utopia!)

How much of their lives do people work for? Maybe they look forward to a long retirement, or maybe they work until they die. Perhaps this is different for different groups in society. And when do they start work? In childhood? Adulthood? Are they allowed to finish their education before gaining employment?

DAY 21: CLASS DIVIDES AND SOCIAL MOBILITY

What sort of class system does your society have? How big is the gap between rich and poor? Maybe the different classes and socio-economic groups live alongside one another, or perhaps they are strictly segregated. How do they view one another, and how do they treat one another?

What chances are there for social mobility? Can someone in your world marry into a higher class? Does education give people a chance to rise up through society? Does employment give them those chances? Perhaps there's something else that can take them up through the ranks of society; something completely unique to your world. Some kind of lottery, or a tournament.

Or, of course, there might be no way at all for your characters to better their situation. Mind you, that won't necessarily stop them from trying.

This is a great source of conflict in your world, and particularly important in dystopian stories. Make sure you're tying it into your culture, and the history of your world.

Prejudice can run deep for many, many generations. What started it? Where and when did it begin? How has it become so ingrained?

DAY 22: RELIGIOUS AND SPIRITUAL BELIEF STRUCTURE

When you're looking at religious and spiritual beliefs in your world, remember that there are probably going to be more than one, and they have probably changed over time. They've been replaced, pushed aside, become old-fashioned. The rites and rituals have changed, parts may have been forgotten, or misinterpreted, or purposefully changed to reflect a changing society, or to fit the agenda of those in charge.

There may be conflict between different religions; causing wars, genocide, changing the government, the laws, and causing huge shockwaves in society. Or, they may rattle alongside one another quite happily, borrowing from one another from time to time.

Creating religions can be a really fun part of worldbuilding; giving you the opportunity to imagine deities, creation stories, festivals, holidays, rites and rituals. You can write songs, poetry, chants, entire scriptures, if you choose.

Think carefully about the day-to-day impact your religion has on your characters; both the believers and the non-believers. Perhaps the calendar revolves around the festivals, perhaps the working week, or the school terms. What impact do the rules and commandments of your religion have? Are they enshrined in law, or are they at odds with the law?

How does it impact the family? Perhaps it heavily influences the educational curriculum, or the punishments dished out for crimes.

Also think about migration of your people. What happens when a new religion is introduced, when they come up against one another?

Remember that religion as an institution is a different thing to someone being religious. Or spiritual. A person can be deeply spiritual, without adhering to the culture of one religion or another. People often pick and choose the parts of a religion that suit them, that back up their beliefs. They are often happy to ignore and sideline the bits that don't suit them.

DAY 23: MAGIC

This can be another really fun part of worldbuilding, but remember: with great power comes great responsibility!

The important thing to bear in mind, when you're building a magic system, is that it has to have limitations. If there are no limitations, then your hero can solve every single problem, every barrier, every conflict with the click of their fingers. Without limitations, you kill off any chance of conflict and tension, effectively killing off your story.

So, let's look at limitations for your magic system. First, you can limit the magic itself. Don't make your characters all powerful. Don't give them every single ability possible. Limit what the magic allows them to do. Perhaps magic manifests differently in different people. Perhaps it is only strong in people during their teenage years. Maybe it only works when the moon is full, or on Thursdays, or when Mars is in retrograde, or whatever you decide.

You can also give your magic system consequences. Maybe using magic tires people out to the point where they can barely stand, or gives them unbearable migraines. Perhaps it prematurely ages them, or removes some of their memories. It might be incredibly complicated to use, and difficult to learn; requiring years of study for even a rudimentary knowledge of it.

Perhaps much of the knowledge has been lost, or needs to be translated from a long-dead language.

Again, also think about the affect it has on day-to-day life. Nothing exists in isolation, and you can change your entire world by simply changing one aspect of it.

Perhaps all education revolves around magic, or the laws are based on it. Maybe they use magic to grow crops, to build houses. Maybe they raise magical animals. Perhaps only certain people are allowed to learn and use magic, and maybe there are harsh punishments for using magic unlicensed.

Use this space to make some notes about magic in your world, and how it fits in with the rest of society. You can also continue with the bonus lesson on building magic systems on page 63.

DAY 24: FESTIVALS AND CELEBRATIONS

Have a look at your world so far, and think about the reasons your people might celebrate with a festival or special holiday. Are they based on agriculture, on the calendar, the sun or moon phases? Perhaps there are religious festivals, or magical festivals. Perhaps they celebrate an important event in history.

There may be celebrations based around rites of passage: comings of age, births, marriages, deaths. Celebrations will exist at a family level, and a local level, and a national level, and, even, an international level.

Think about how these festivals are celebrated. Which traditions are upheld, and which have been abandoned? Consider what foods might be available, the kind of entertainment they would have, the level of technology.

Does everyone get to celebrate? Does the whole of society shut down for the celebrations? Because of their job, there are likely to be those who have no choice but to continue working through the holidays. But, there may also be people who are barred from the festivities.

Are there festivals that are divisive, and cause conflict? Festivals that attract protests, or that have been outlawed altogether?

DAY 25: TECHNOLOGY

What is the level of technology that exists in your world? Even when you're writing a fantasy set in a medieval-type setting, they can still have technology and knowledge that outstrips ours today. Many ancient civilisations had technology and invented things that would amaze us, and many of them had technology and knowledge that has been forgotten. Some of their achievements are still beyond our understanding.

While they may not have electric lights and the internet, they might have something fantastical and beyond our own abilities. They might have technology run by magic, or be able to harness the power of the moon and stars. They might rely on fire, or steam, or gas, or lightning.

You may be writing about a futuristic world, in which case, you need to invent your own technology. Look at the technological advancements of the last few generations. Look at where the interest is. Look at the trends, and try to project them to your future world. And don't be scared about getting it wrong. You're writing about a *possible* future, there's no need to accurately predict it!

Just keep bringing it back to the single question of what makes sense in your world. And look at the impact of technology on the lives of your characters. Does it enhance their lives, or is it invasive? Is it available, accessible, and affordable for everyone? Has it replaced jobs, or changed the way people live their lives? How has it impacted different people, and groups of people, both positively and negatively?

DAY 26: MEDICINE

Just like technology, it's not necessarily the case that historic worlds have lesser knowledge or advancement than we do today. They might have a different understanding of things, and knowledge far better than ours.

They might practice medicine based on religion, or use natural remedies. They might use magic, or music, or chanting, or hypnosis. They might use lasers, or cloning, or 3D printing.

Beyond thinking about the basis of scientific and medical knowledge, you also need to think about its place in society. Do different groups of people use different forms of medicine? And what would happen if someone fell ill in another area, where medicine was totally different?

Can everyone access medicine? Perhaps some people will rush to their local state-of-the-art hospital, while others will turn to an elder in their village. Maybe conventional medicine is incredibly expensive. Perhaps alternative therapies suddenly grow in popularity, pushing up the prices of what was once a cheap, local choice.

Who can practice medicine? Is this a world where local midwives and wise-women have to live under the radar, fearful of being found out? Is it a world where women can rise quickly through the ranks of the medical field? Where training and qualifications in medicine are subsidised by the government, and taught in universities that actively seek to recruit students from disadvantaged backgrounds?

DAY 27: WEAPONRY

What weapons exist in your world? Perhaps your characters fight with swords and axes, attacking on horseback, or on foot. Perhaps they use guns, tanks, bombs. Maybe they use magic or laser guns.

The weaponry in your world will be closely connected to the level of technology that you're introducing. But, what happens if an army invades with a different level of technology? A different kind of weaponry?

Who has access to weapons? Who has the training to wield them? Maybe there are weapons that have been banned, or weapons that can be illegally adapted. Maybe there are weapons that can no longer be used because the knowledge or ability to use them has been lost.

Think about how weaponry links to your society. Why do they favour one weapon over another? What restrictions or features of your world have forced this choice? What skills and talents of your people?

Also consider society's attitudes towards weapons. Are they carried openly, or concealed? Are the military a common sight in the city, or are they rarely seen? Think about whether your police are armed, and what proportion of the general public are. Do people act with surprise when they see weapons, or are they an everyday sight?

DAY 28: HISTORIC WARS

Everything in your world is shaped by its past. What scars remain from wars fought in your world? What monuments and reminders are there?

It may be streets named after famous generals, or battles. It may be cities built around a central war memorial. It might be towns with very few men left.

Wars can change huge things in your world: borders, governments, languages, religions, freedoms. It can bring slavery, new technologies, an influx of immigrants, or an outpouring of refugees (who then become immigrants elsewhere).

Think about the historic wars that have happened in your world, the affect that they have had, and the reminders that remain.

Also consider the attitudes of society towards these wars. Are they spoken of with a sense of national pride, or whispered about shamefully? Are people still angry, or mourning? How are soldiers treated, and how are injured soldiers treated? How about those who desert or get discharged?

DAY 29: SOCIAL CHANGE AND REVOLUTION

Your world may have also seen big changes via a rise-up of the people. These don't, necessarily, have to be violent uprisings. There may have been policy changes brought about diplomatically. Peacefully.

What changes has society seen in your world, and how have they been brought about? Did people sacrifice themselves for the greater good, throwing themselves onto the sword to bring about change? Or did they fight from the inside; rising up through government to reforge the world?

What reminders of these events still remain? Perhaps there are streets named after the great protestors, or festivals to recognise their sacrifice. Maybe gallows still stand in the city as a warning to those who might start thinking revolutionary thoughts.

How have things been changed for your people? What freedoms have been won and lost?

Perhaps, the revolution is still to come...

DAY 30: OTHER HISTORIC EVENTS

What other events have shaped your world? Volcanoes, earthquakes, climate change, the death of the sun. Plagues, invasions, an apocalypse, an extinction.

Perhaps something happened that changed the evolution of the land, or the people, entirely. Maybe something occurred that set the world off on a totally different course.

Again; think about how these events have shaped your world into what it has become. And think about how it has affected the people, and their lives.

Congratulations! You are now a deity in your own right, able to sit back and proudly survey the world that you have created. You've moulded it with your own hands from nothing. You imagined it, and now, here it is. Fresh, and new, and wonderful.

Look closely. Can you see all those little people walking about down there? They're the important ones. And you're about to give them one hell of an adventure.

They are the ones that matter. When you're building your world, you always need to bring it back to the people. How things affect them, and their lives.

Because, that's who your story is about. Its characters.

Always remember that you are not writing about a wondrous world in which some characters happen to live. You are writing about wondrous characters who happen to live in the world you've built for them.

BONUS: CREATING A MAGIC SYSTEM

Magic can come in many different forms; from a little unexplained intuition, or a skill for fortune telling, right up to epic battles between wizards and warlords.

It may be something that exists, quietly, alongside the story, or it may be the very crux of the story itself. Magic might have been forgotten, or lost, or outlawed. It might be dying out, or it may be reappearing in youngsters for the first time in centuries.

Magic might be revered in your world, with those able to practice it gaining status and power. It may be feared, or persecuted, or kept secret. It might exist as public knowledge, it might be completely unknown to the majority, or explained away as something else.

Is it part of a conspiracy, or a way to control the people? Or is it their only hope of freedom, and the power behind an uprising?

However magic is used, or exists in your world, and whatever form it takes, there are some principles to building a magic system that are universal.

1: GENRE

Your magic system will work best when it is tied closely to the story, the characters, and the world.

Think, first, about the genre of your book. There is no rule that says magic can only exist in fantasy novels, and it frequently makes an appearance in science-fiction, horror, and many other genres. The genre of your story can help to inform what kind of magic system you create.

If you're writing a steampunk story, you might base your magic in mechanics, or plumbing, or fire. If you're writing an epic fantasy, it might be nature-based magic, in urban-fantasy, it might be based on the moon. If you're putting magic into a futuristic setting, it might be closely linked with technology and science.

Write down the genre of your story, and the genre elements and conventions you plan to include. Look at ways in which you can tie your magic system to these things.

2: SETTING

There are many ways that you can tie your magic system to your setting.

Think about the resources needed for magic. Do they need herbs and roots? Do they need to be able to see the stars clearly? Do they need to be near water, or rock, or ice? Are there places that enhance and strengthen their magic, and places that dampen and dull it?

You can use settings as a way to assist the magic, as well as a way to hamper it. Perhaps magic cannot travel through rock. Perhaps it is useless in a blizzard. Perhaps the lights of the city block out the stars, or a particular herb is rare and expensive.

Maybe, when people with magical powers are arrested, they need special cells to stop their magic from working. Perhaps magicians require access to magical fighting arenas which are few and far between.

Write down some settings that will appear in your story, and think about how they might help the magic, giving it the resources it needs, and think about how it might make magic more difficult, or entirely ineffective.

3: CHARACTER

Absolutely everything in your story and your worldbuilding should always come back to character. They are the reason your readers stick with the story. They always need to be central to everything.

There are many ways in which you can tie your magic system to character.

What kind of people are able to practice magic? Is it available to everyone, or only to some? If only some people can practice magic, why is that? Perhaps it's nature; that only certain races have magical powers. Or only specific genders, or ages, or perhaps it's genetic, or completely random. Maybe some people aren't allowed to practice magic based on society's laws, or maybe they are barred from it for other reasons: geographical, socio-economic, physical limitations, etc.

What is the everyday affect that magic has on their life? Does it affect the school they go to, the friends they have, and their leisure activities? Does it give them status in society, or make them the subject of ridicule, fear, or punishment?

What sacrifices does your character have to make for their magic? Perhaps they've had to say goodbye to their friends, their family, their home, their freedom. Maybe they've had to give up on their childhood, or any hope of having a 'normal' life. How do they feel about magic?

Write down some ways in which magic has changed your character's life, both good and bad. Think about how it impacts their motivations and goals. How it helps them to overcome obstacles, and how it creates obstacles itself.

4: SOCIETY

As well as affecting your characters' lives individually, magic also affects, and is affected by, society as a whole.

Think about the different aspects of your society and the part that magic plays in them: education, industry, government, food and farming, trade, religion, economics, medicine, defence.

Magic might be the very cornerstone of your society. It might form the basis of education, the laws may be based on magic, the religion, the technology. It might permeate every part of society.

Or, perhaps it's kept strictly separate. Perhaps they're not allowed to teach magic in schools. Perhaps magic isn't spoken of, and books on magic are removed from libraries. Are those books burnt, or are they hoarded away in private collections?

Also think about how things have changed over the last few decades, or centuries. Maybe magic is being removed from society; laws changed, magic dropping off the school timetable, doctors abandoning magic in favour of modern medicine. Or maybe its influence is strengthening. For better or worse, think about the changing influence magic has had in your society.

Write down some notes about the position magic holds in your world. Remember this may be different in different places, or for different groups of people.

5: MAGICAL ITEMS

While magic may be practised by, simply, a twist of a hand, there are still likely to be artefacts and items important for its use, or important to its history.

Your magic system may require certain items to work at all; wands, mirrors, blades, herbs, rings, metals. Or these items may be ceremonial, needed for the rites and rituals to be carried out as per tradition.

Your magic system may have important texts and documents, necessary for a full understanding of it.

Think about the rarity, the value, and the cost of these items. Think about who has access to them, and who they are kept from. How dangerous are they, and what protections might someone need to handle them?

Are there items that have been lost over time? Or broken? Or stolen? And how has magic changed without their availability?

Maybe there are items that exist in myth and legend, with some devoting their lives to searching for them, while others deny their existence entirely.

What would someone be willing to sacrifice to find, to keep, or to destroy an item?

6: LIMITATIONS

Your magic system should have limitations. If magic is limitless and all powerful, if magic can be easily used to solve every problem your characters face, then your scope for creating conflict in your story is much reduced.

If your magic system has limits, or your character's use or knowledge of it has limits, then you can still put obstacles in the way of them achieving their goal. You can give them struggles, and put them in danger, and leave your readers wondering whether or not they will succeed.

Think about some ways in which your magic can be limited, or your character's use of it may be limited. Give your magic system rules and guidelines.

Perhaps magic only works under a full moon, or in open air. Perhaps it can't cure wounds, or mend machines. Maybe it requires silence and concentration to perform. Maybe each spell takes weeks of preparation.

Create some limitations for your magic system, remembering to think about all of the things you've already written about it. Fit the limitations into your world just as carefully as you've fitted the magic itself. It all needs to tie together.

7: CONSEQUENCES

As well as limitations on the magic itself, you can also raise the stakes, and the tension, by creating consequences for using magic.

These could be legal consequences; if they are likely to be arrested or tortured for publicly using magic. Perhaps they are faced with a dilemma where they need to use magic to save someone they love, but by doing so, they are condemning themselves to a death sentence.

The consequences could be physical; with magic usage making your character tired, or weak, or knocking them unconscious. Perhaps it makes them sick, or they only have a certain amount of magic to use before it runs out completely. Maybe they have to drop their defences in order to attack, leaving them vulnerable.

There may be moral consequences too; magic may work in a state of balance, meaning that, if your character uses magic to save a life, another is taken elsewhere. Or, if they use magic to halt a flood, another town is swamped with water. Perhaps all magic sent out into the world is returned to the user three-fold.

Write down some consequences for using magic, whether it affects just the individual, or has a wider impact.

8: WORKING WITH MORE THAN ONE MAGIC SYSTEM

You may decide that you want more than one magic system in your world. These varying kinds of magic may be practised by people in different areas, or different races, different genders, socio-economic groups, or species.

It may be a free choice, as to which magic system a person chooses to follow. Maybe they are encouraged down a particular magical path based on their competencies and talents. Maybe it's based on their family's traditions. Perhaps some magic systems are thought of as high-brow and respectable, while others are viewed as common and lowly.

Different magic systems may be exclusive, with each person only ever able, or allowed, to follow one path. Or they may be more integrated, borrowing from one another, with people able to create their own magic mash-ups.

If you decide to include more than one magic system, simply work through these prompts for each system you wish to include, and then spend some time considering how they work, or don't work, alongside one another.

The clashes between different magic systems may be violent and divisive. They might bring about struggles for power, or genocide, or war. They may exist respectfully alongside one another. They might complement each other, working together to create a more powerful magic overall.

A WORD ON INFO DUMPING AND LEARNING CURVES

Once you have completed your worldbuilding, and you are ready to start writing your book, you need to consider how, and how much, of this information to include.

Don't think that you will be including every ounce of what you've worked on. You won't. You shouldn't. I know, I know, you worked hard on it, but it wasn't wasted, even if it never makes it into your book. It helped you to understand your world, so that you can write about it in an informed, attached, and immersive way. So that you can make it all the more real for your readers.

An 'info dump' is the term used for when a writer pours out information onto the page as if they are writing a history text book. It's dry, it's dull, and, more often than not, it's confusing.

I'm sure you will have heard the old adage 'show don't tell'. This means that you should be *showing* your readers your worldbuilding, through action and dialogue, not simply *telling* them via a historical lecture.

The absolute best way to teach your readers about your world, is through action. This might be your character clashing with police, or it may simply be them navigating the world.

Let me expand on that: if something in your world is absolutely normal, however far removed it is from our world, if you character treats it, and reacts to it, as if it is entirely regular and everyday, then you are teaching your readers about your world through action.

Say, for example, centaurs are a common sight in your world. If your character treats them with no surprise at all, talking to them as if they are another human, then your readers learn that centaurs and humans live alongside one another equally. Or, perhaps your character ridicules, or bullies the centaurs. Or they treat them with respect, or fear. This is what you are teaching your readers about what is the norm in your world. Through action. This is the ideal way to show your worldbuilding.

It's not always so easy.

And so, the next best way is through dialogue. Again, avoid huge blocks of information. This is no different to info dumping, you're simply letting the history lecture come out of a character's mouth. However, they can have a conversation with a friend about a historical aspect of the world, or a cultural aspect. A conversation. Not a lecture.

Sometimes, however, you need to break the rules.

I'm not saying that you must never simply tell your readers information. Sometimes, it's necessary. Sometimes, it's even the better option. But, do it with careful consideration, and do it sparingly. Rules are, certainly in creative pursuits, meant to be broken.

If you're concerned about whether or not you're getting the balance right, the best way is through the use of beta readers. Beta readers read through early, pre-publication versions of books, and give honest feedback that allows the author to improve their story. If you've got the balance wrong, beta readers can tell you.

Another way to learn this is through reading, reading, and reading. Take careful note of how other authors handle the dilemma. How they get the balance right, and how they get it wrong.

The other way is simply through practice. The more you write, the more you drill down into your personal style and voice, the better you are likely to get at it.

The way in which you give worldbuilding information to your readers also depends on the complexity of your world, and how different it is to ours.

If you're writing about earth, whether in the present, past, or future, there are many things your readers will already know. They understand about time, and seasons. They know the animals, the plants. They know what humans are like, and how they interact. The learning curve of your world may be quite a gentle one.

Everything in your world that is different to our real world, adds to the learning curve of your book. Every mythical creature, every imagined technology, every drop of magic, and every jargon word makes that curve a little bit steeper.

You want to ease your readers in. If, in chapter one, you expect them to learn everything about your world and its history, learn who the characters are, and absorb their struggles and goals, they will be exhausted by the time they get to chapter two.

Tell them what they need to know. They don't need 5 million years worth of military history. They may need flashes of it, but not the entire thing. Be gentle with them. Don't make them do too much work, and don't leave them floundering around your story loaded down with too much knowledge.

Again, these are things that you can learn and improve on with the help of beta readers, by reading, reading, reading, and by simply practising your craft. You will find your way, I promise, but I can't tell you how to do it, because we are all different. And our stories are different. And our voices are different.

You might write short, 50,000 word novels, and leave a lot of the deeper worldbuilding out. You might write 130,000 word epics, with readers who expect a much more immersive experience. Practice, experiment, and you'll find the right balance for you, your books, and your readers.

IDEAS DUMP

As you work your way through this book, you are bound to have flashes of ideas popping into your mind. Character and story ideas, that don't quite belong with the workbook prompts.

Don't lose them; those little flashes are important.

Instead, use the following pages as something of an ideas dump. Some of these may never make it into your finished book, but, you never know, you may be able to recycle them into other stories.

No idea is ever wasted...

WANT EVEN MORE WORLDBUILDING?

Our adventures don't have to end here...

You can explore the rest of my series of worldbuilding guides for authors, guiding you through the basics of worldbuilding, helping you to create magic systems and religions, to write dystopian and post-apocalyptic fiction, and to create histories rich with myths and monsters.

Find more information on all of my workbooks and other worldbuilding services at angelinetrevena.co.uk/worldbuilding

Get Your Free Creating a Timeline Worksheet

Join my worldbuilding mailing list to claim your free Creating a Timeline worksheet.

You will also receive all the latest news on releases and workshops, as well as worldbuilding tips, tricks, and resources.

Join at subscribepage.com/worldbuilding

ABOUT ANGELINE TREVENA

Angeline Trevena was born and bred in a rural corner of Devon, but now lives among the breweries and canals of central England with her husband, their two sons, and a rather neurotic cat. She is a dystopian urban fantasy and post-apocalyptic author, a podcaster, and events manager.

In 2003 she graduated from Edge Hill University, Lancashire, with a BA Hons Degree in Drama and Writing. During this time she decided that her future lay in writing words rather than performing them.

Some years ago she worked at an antique auction house and religiously checked every wardrobe that came in to see if Narnia was in the back of it. She's still not given up looking for it.

Find out more at www.angelinetrevena.co.uk

Made in the USA
Las Vegas, NV
27 January 2022